D1643399

LIVES OF IRISH ARTISTS

Leech

William Leech
1881-1968

DENISE FERRAN

LIVES OF IRISH ARTISTS

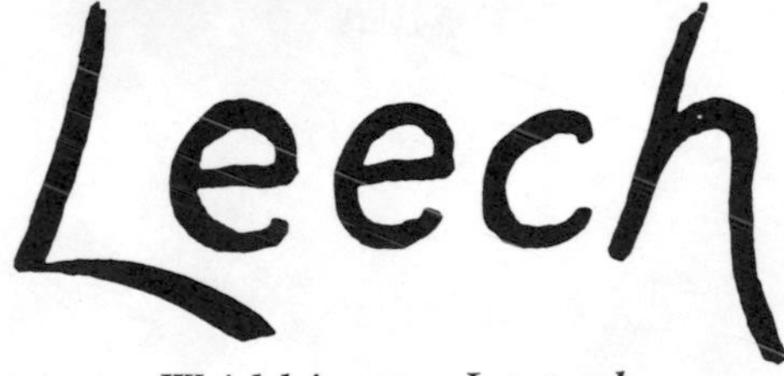

William Leech
1881-1968

To Sean for all the support
Denise

DENISE FERRAN

TOWN HOUSE, DUBLIN
IN ASSOCIATION WITH
THE NATIONAL GALLERY OF IRELAND

Published in 1992 by
Town House
42 Morehampton Road
Donnybrook
Dublin 4
in association with The National Gallery of Ireland

British Library Cataloguing in Publication Data
Ferran, Denise
William Leech, 1881-1968.— (Lives of Irish Artists Series)
I. Title II. Series
759.2915

ISBN: 0-948524-35-9

Cover: *Quimperlé — The Goose-Girl c* 1911
Title page: Photo of Leech courtesy The Ulster Museum

Managing editor: Treasa Coady
Series editor: Brian P Kennedy (NGI)
Text editors: Elaine Campion, Bernie Daly
Colour origination: The Kulor Centre
Design concept: Q Design
Printed in Hong Kong

CONTENTS

ILLUSTRATIONS

Denise Ferran is art education officer at the Ulster Museum, Belfast. An art history graduate of the Courtauld Institute of London University, she holds a diploma in Advanced Studies in Education from Queen's University Belfast, and is completing a doctoral thesis at Trinity College Dublin. She is a practising painter and has won the silver medal and the watercolour prize at the Royal Ulster Academy. She has illustrated a number of books and has written diverse catalogue texts.

❧

William John Leech considered himself an Irish painter but his parents' move to London from Dublin in 1910 lessened his contact with Ireland. It is likely that he returned only once for a short visit, but he exhibited about three hundred paintings at the Royal Hibernian Academy during his long career. His early work in Ireland consisted of family portraits and landscapes, including views of Killiney. Brittany inspired his painting and brought light and colour into his work. Although he was initially devoted to French painters, from the 1930s his work became more influenced by the English school of painting.

CHILDHOOD IN DUBLIN

William John Leech was born on 10 April 1881 at 49 Rutland Square, Dublin, the third son of Henry Brougham Leech and his wife Anne Louise (née Garbois). His father was registrar of deeds and regius professor of law at Trinity College Dublin. There were six children in the family. The first five were boys, all born at Rutland Square, and the youngest child and only daughter, Kathleen, was born in 1889, the year after the Leech family had moved to Yew Park, Clontarf.

William John or Bill, as he was known in the family circle, followed his two older brothers, Arthur and Harry, to St Columba's College, Rathfarnham, in 1893. Unlike his brothers Leech showed little interest in academic studies and after four years he was sent to study French in Switzerland, where he spent a year becoming a fluent French speaker. In 1898, at the age of seventeen, he enrolled at the Metropolitan School of Art in Dublin, breaking the family tradition of studying at Trinity

College Dublin. He wrote in later life about his early art school experience: 'Orpen had just left for the Slade, everyone was talking about him and old Brenan (the Headmaster) used to call me a second Orpen.'

Leech spent only one year at the Metropolitan School before transferring to the Royal Hibernian Academy schools, where he studied for two years. He later observed: 'Walter Osborne was a visiting master, he had enthusiasm and could teach. It was about then that I first saw French painting, the Impressionists etc., what a sudden revelation. Doors and windows thrown open and the darkness invaded by light and air, it was the beginning for me.' The Leech family was an established Anglo-Irish Protestant one, happy and close-knit, and they supported Bill's artistic ambitions. A Swiss landscape entitled *Lake Brienz before a Storm* was the first work he exhibited at the Royal Hibernian Academy in 1899, when he was eighteen years old. His youngest brother, Freddie, who died tragically in 1906 while still a law student at Trinity College, recognised his brother's talent and predicted: 'Our family name will be remembered because of Billie's pictures.'

A Student in Paris

In 1901 William Leech enrolled at the Académie Julian in Paris. His father found him comfortable lodgings with an Irish landlady, but he left these to share a studio with his two new friends from New Zealand, Sydney Thompson and Charles Bickerton. Leech later described this Montparnasse studio as frugal: 'It was a small studio in the Rue Beloni, away up behind the Gare Montparnasse and very bleak, no curtains, the bleak north light and skylight stretching right across it. Furniture? — a deal table, two or three kitchen chairs, a gallery to sleep in, no beds, just a mattress on the floor.' Leech was fastidious about his appearance, trimmed his moustache and looked more like a businessman than a Parisian artist. He was handsome, charming and soft spoken. As a student he applied himself to his studies, working diligently at drawing from life. He soon received praiseworthy mention for his drawing in Julian's monthly magazine *Concours*. He recalled in later life that 'we worked very hard at the school from 8 am till noon, then from 1 pm till 4 pm, of course one learned a lot, drawing and painting the nude'.

In addition to Jean-Paul Laurens, one of Leech's visiting tutors was William Bouguereau, who was then elderly. A standing male figure, which Leech painted while a student in Laurens' studio, demonstrates that he was a very able draughtsman and an accomplished academic painter. He was quickly accepted by the French students because of his fluent French and was popular because he acted as an interpreter for his English-speaking friends. Although he had already exhibited at the Royal Hibernian Academy in 1899, he did not exhibit his paintings during his student years. While in Paris he won his first Taylor prize and was subsequently awarded two Taylor scholarships in 1905 and 1906. When the academies closed for the summer months Leech's fellow students flocked out of Paris, seeking unspoilt areas where they could paint in the open air. Leech, in contrast, returned to the comfort of the large family home at Clontarf in Dublin.

❧

The Brittany Years, 1903–14

Leech's father had given him a sum of money and commissioned his son to paint family portraits to help establish his career. Instead of returning to the Académie Julian in Paris in the autumn of 1903, Leech was persuaded by his friend Sydney Thompson to go with him to Concarneau in Brittany, where Thompson had been living for some time. This move was to have the most important influence on Leech's painting career. Here he became absorbed by the surroundings, painting the harbour, the old town and the boats, and he exhibited pictures of many of the scenes in Dublin. Concarneau, with its old walled town, the harbour with its tuna and sardine fishing, and the colourful markets frequented by the local peasants in their traditional Breton costumes, was well loved by artists, and it became the particular inspiration for Leech's landscape paintings until 1917.

When Leech first arrived in Brittany, he painted in a formal academic manner, using earth tones and a restricted palette. It was not until five years later that his palette lightened and his brushwork became more confident and fluid. He exhibited at the Royal Hibernian Academy from 1903 onwards, and in 1909 one of the eight paintings he exhibited was *Interior of a Café* (*Pl 1*). He also showed this again in 1910 at the Royal Institute of Oil Painters in London. This work, for which Leech made studies, is in the style of popular nineteenth-century French realism and is reminiscent of early Orpen. It was probably painted in the café of the Hôtel des Voyageurs in Concarneau, where he was then living. The peasants in the painting would have been familiar to Leech as he had by then spent five years painting in Concarneau. He had already painted the rugged peasant, seated on the left, in a similar pose in 1904, indicating that *Interior of a Café* was built up from individual studies painted over a period of time and composed into the final studio painting. A second version of this work,

cont. p25

ILLUSTRATIONS

PLATE 1

Interior of a Café 1908

Pl 1

This early work, painted in Brittany, is one of the few Leech dated, and is in the style of French realism. It was probably painted in the café of the Hôtel des Voyageurs in Concarneau, where Leech stayed. Four years previously, he had painted an individual study of the peasant who is seated to the left.

Oil on canvas; 74 x 84 cm
Private collection

Pl 2

The ramparts of the walled town of Concarneau are reflected in the sunlit water of the harbour where a sardine boat is being prepared for a fishing trip. Light pervades Leech's canvas and the soft tones of the painting show the influence of Whistler, although the high horizon line and fluid brush-strokes owe more to John Lavery, with whom he was acquainted.

Oil on canvas; 56 x 82 cm
National Gallery of Ireland

Pl 3

Leech travelled frequently by train from Concarneau to nearby Quimperlé where Walter Osborne, his teacher in Dublin, had painted Apple Gathering, Quimperlé *(National Gallery of Ireland) in 1883. The influence of Osborne and of Bastien-Lepage is apparent in the style of the brush-strokes, the high horizon line formed by the sunlit meadow of flowers, and the upright figure of the goose-girl.*

Oil on canvas; 72 x 91 cm
National Gallery of Ireland

PLATE 2

Waving Things, Concarneau 1910

PLATE 3

Quimperlé — The Goose-Girl *c* 1911

PLATE 4

A Convent Garden, Brittany *c* 1911

Pl 4 *Elizabeth Saurine Kerlin, Leech's first wife, was the model for many of his paintings. Here she poses in a convent garden, wearing a traditional Breton wedding dress and bonnet. This picture was painted about the time of their marriage in 1912. Leech originally gave the painting the title* Les Soeurs du St Esprit, *the name of the order of nuns who ran the hospital in the old walled town of Concarneau.*

Oil on canvas; 132 x 106 cm
National Gallery of Ireland

Pl 5

Elizabeth is portrayed here as an elegant and beautiful woman in a pose and style reminiscent of Orpen. The cigarette in her raised right hand is a statement about the increasing freedom sought by fashionable women at that time, to be able to smoke and to vote. Elizabeth was a young, aspiring painter when Leech first met her in France.

Oil on canvas; 66 x 42 cm
Hugh Lane Municipal Gallery of Modern Art, Dublin

Pl 6

In 1919, just after the war, Leech met May Botterell in London. This portrait, commissioned by her husband Percy Botterell, was exhibited at the Paris Salon in 1922, where it was awarded a bronze medal. It shows the elegant wife of a successful lawyer, in a fashionable evening dress. The pose and oriental style of the figure emulates Whistler.

Oil on canvas; 121.9 x 121.9 cm
Private collection

PLATE 5

The Cigarette *c* 1915

PLATE 6

Portrait of Mrs May Botterell *c* 1920

PLATE 7

Aloes *c* 1922

Pl 7

Leech began to paint his series of large cacti when he visited Les Martiques, near Aix-en-Provence, in 1917/18. From this time on he divided his time between London and the south of France.

Oil on canvas; 181 x 148.3 cm
Ulster Museum, Belfast

PLATE 8

Chrysanthemums *c* 1940

Pl 8

Colour, light, pattern and composition are all effectively incorporated into this still-life painting, making an impressive work out of a simple window ledge, on which sits a vase of chrysanthemums. The diagonal sweep of the window, the reflected and refracted shadows imbued with colour, and the confident brush-strokes are characteristic of Leech's mature style.

Oil on canvas; 56 x 45.5 cm
AIB collection

PLATE 9

Au Cinquième: A Portrait of the Artist's Wife *c* 1940

Pl 9

In this painting Leech has encapsulated a gentle domesticity. May Botterell is seen reading a book at the window of her fifth floor flat at 20 Abbey Road, London. Though he captures May's likeness with ease and accuracy, Leech is more fascinated by the play of light on her neck, hand and sweater. This painting was exhibited at the Royal Hibernian Academy in 1967, and Leech expressed his disappointment 'that none of the critics mentioned Au Cinquième, *I suppose it was badly hung, I think it one of my best things'.*

Oil on canvas; 74 x 60 cm
National Gallery of Ireland

Pl 10

This self-portrait is one of a series which Leech painted just two years before he died, when he was in his eighty-sixth year. He used a large mirror in his studio to capture his image, and his painting of Aloes (Pl 7) *is reflected in reverse behind him. This picture was painted in his last studio, built in the garden of Candy Cottage near Guildford, Surrey, which he bought with May after their marriage in 1953.*

Oil on canvas; 64 x 56 cm
National Gallery of Ireland

PLATE 10

A Self-Portrait c 1965

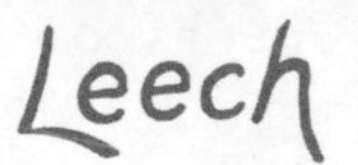

cont. from p12

Le Café des Artistes — Concarneau was awarded the bronze medal at the Paris Salon in 1914.

Leech's early Brittany paintings were academic, and those exhibited at the Royal Hibernian Academy in 1906 were referred to by a Dublin critic as 'Mr Leech's "brown studies" '. But, in painting the boats in the harbour and the people at work in the markets, and by working *en plein air*, Leech's painting changed and his canvases became flooded with light. In his painting *Waving Things, Concarneau* (*Pl 2*), Leech shows an awareness of the soft tonalities of Whistler's landscape paintings. This work, shown in his one-man exhibition at the Baillie Gallery in London in 1911, is similar in style to the atmospheric paintings included in Leech's one-man exhibition at the Goupil Gallery, London, in 1912, entitled *Visions of Switzerland, Venice, etc.* Leech had already exhibited in the Goupil Gallery with Orpen in 1911, and the scale of this one-man exhibition indicates Leech's serious intent as an artist. His work then showed the influence not only of Whistler but also of Lavery. The review of the exhibition in *The Times* refers to Leech as 'an artist who aims at vivid illusion by means of that process of elimination which was practised by Whistler'.

Leech's parents had moved from Dublin to London in 1910, and from then until his father's death in 1921 he divided his time between London and France, using his parents' London home as his address in England. His parents' move facilitated the exhibition of his work in

London, although he continued to show at the Royal Hibernian Academy, being elected an academician in 1910 after Dermod O'Brien became president. In Dublin each August, between 1907 and 1910, he showed in a group exhibition at the Leinster Lecture Hall in Molesworth Street, with Casimir Dunin-Markievicz, Constance Gore-Booth, A E Russell and Dermod O'Brien, who was a powerful advocate for Leech's work. In 1910 he exhibited for the first time in London, at the Royal Academy, followed by a comprehensive exhibition in the Baillie Gallery in January 1911. *The Times'* critic wrote about this exhibition: 'there are some good oil pictures, landscapes and portraits by Mr W J Leech, an artist of much promise, ... '. From 1910 onwards colour and sunlight permeate Leech's canvases, especially when he incorporates figures into his landscapes. This is evident in *Summer Brittany,* where a Breton woman and a young girl lean against a bridge in front of a gentle flowing river, with houses in the background, evoking Quimperlé. The woman's bonnet, painted in soft orange, parallels the vibrant splash of sunlit orange in the long dress of *The Goose-Girl* (*Pl 3*), which was probably painted at the same time and in the same location. Flocks of geese, tended by a young girl, were a familiar sight in the countryside. The figure in this picture bears a strong resemblance to Elizabeth Saurine Kerlin (née Lane), who was the attractive, American-born model for many of his works at the time. She is also the young novice, dressed in the glistening white traditional gown and starched coiffe of a Breton bride, who glides across the bright yellow grass, enriched with tall, white lilies, in *A Convent Garden, Brittany* (*Pl 4*). This painting glows with light and colour, and moving in the background shadows of the tree-lined avenue in the walled garden are the nuns, 'Les Soeurs du St Esprit', who ran the hospital in Concarneau where Leech had convalesced from typhoid fever. *The Sunshade* also belongs to this period. Elizabeth, whom he married in 1912, is again the model, and the background is Leech's painting of a garden of lilies. The lilies became the foreground of *A Convent Garden, Brittany,* and in *The Sunshade* they give the impression that the model posed in a garden rather than in a studio.

❧

THE GREAT WAR

Leech's confidence and reputation as a painter was growing, but with the outbreak of the First World War in 1914 his life and his style of painting changed. During the war he painted in France, mainly in Paris but also in Brittany and Provence. *The Cigarette* (*Pl 5*) dates from this period. Light comes from the left and falls onto the beautiful face of Elizabeth, who is seated in a fashionabl pose with her raised right hand holding a cigarette. There are similarities in style and composition between this painting of Elizabeth in her black satin dress, and portraits by John Lavery, with whom Leech was acquainted. Leech has carefully rendered the lacy pattern of the white blouse, in contrast to the smoothness of the black satin in the dress. The vase to the right, framed against the painting in the background, shows the influence of Whistler and of Japanese art. *The Tinsel Scarf* (Hugh Lane Municipal Gallery of Modern Art, Dublin) which depicts Elizabeth draped languidly across a couch, wearing a decorative shawl, also belongs to this period in Paris. Towards the end of the war, in 1917, Leech went with his friend Sydney Thompson to Les Martiques, near Aix-en-Provence in the south of France, where he began painting, *en plein air*, pictures of aloes, large cactus plants. This happy period ended when Leech was called up in the spring of 1918, and he spent the remaining six months of the war in a detention camp in France. On returning to his parents' London home, he was in a very depressed state. His marriage to Elizabeth had become strained, he had sold very few paintings, he was penniless and he found himself unable to paint.

❧

Leech

Portrait of Mrs Botterell

Leech was introduced to the Botterell family in 1919 by his brother Cecil, a full-time officer in the British Army. Percy Botterell, an eminent London lawyer, helped Leech by commissioning him to paint his portrait, and also to paint one of his wife May. This large portrait of May, in an elegant blue evening gown, was exhibited as *The Blue Portrait* at the Irish Art Exhibition in Brussels in May 1920, and also as *Portrait of Mrs May Botterell* (*Pl 6*) at the Royal Academy exhibition in January 1921. It won Leech a bronze medal at the Paris Salon in 1922. In 1921 both of Leech's parents died. His sister Kathleen, who had married the Reverend Charles Cox and was living in the north of England, continued to support him, as did many other members of his family. Leech stayed with Kathleen for extended periods each year, painting the landscape around the vicarage, particularly the railway line and the telegraph poles which ran alongside. This fascination with the dramatic sweep and pattern of railway tracks remained one of his subjects until the early 1960s. *Railway Embankment* (Ulster Museum) captures the play of sunlight on the fencing and grassy embankment in a dramatic composition. Leech continued to visit his sister each year, and he gave the Cox family paintings in return for his keep. He also painted portraits of each member of the family, capturing their likeness with ease and confidence.

Leech's chance meeting with May Botterell changed the course of both their lives. She was an elegant, rich, cultured woman who became Leech's life-long support, both emotionally and financially, especially after the death of his parents. Leech got to know her three children and he painted their portraits. An appearance of normal life was maintained, with May living at home in Hampstead with her family, looking after her children and continuing as wife and social hostess. During the day she left her comfortable home to visit Leech and share his more Bohemian life in his studio nearby. Only when the children had grown up did May move out to her flat in Abbey Road, but she still maintained close links with her husband and children, sharing holidays with them. Leech and Mrs Botterell avoided any hint of a scandal, but this avoidance of publicity curtailed the exhibition of Leech's paintings.

Mrs Botterell and Leech divided their time between London and the south of France, where they went for several months in the spring of each year. In the 1920s Leech had rented a house at St Jennet, where he continued his friendship with the Thompson family who were living nearby. When he painted in the bright light of the south of France, light, colour and pattern again flooded into his pictures. He continued to paint aloes, which he had first painted in 1917 at Les Martiques and which he again painted at Grasse in the 1920s. *Aloes* (*Pl* 7) is a large painting in the series, with the stiff leaves forming upright shapes against a sloping field of sunlight and colour. The backgrounds, painted in short diagonal brush-strokes of brilliant colour, contrast with the more formal shapes of the cactus leaves. *Un Matin* (Hugh Lane Municipal Gallery, Dublin) was painted as part of the same series. Leech presented this work to the Dublin Gallery in memory of Hugh Lane who had drowned in 1915 in the *Lusitania* disaster.

London and Steele's Studio

When away from the sun and heat of the south of France, Leech still incorporated the pattern and colour of the aloes series in his paintings of flowers, especially of chrysanthemums and daisies, and these qualities are all present in his painting *Chrysanthemums* (*Pl 8*). May was fond of flowers and these became a recurring still-life theme. He painted at Steele's Studio in Hampstead from 1928 until it was damaged by a bomb in 1941, when his address became 20 Abbey Road. This had been May's flat since 1938 and Leech frequently painted portraits of friends there, such as the writer Aldous Huxley's aunt, *Mrs Huxley Roller*, an artist who exhibited at the Royal Academy. Through May's circle of London friends, Leec became familiar with a group of intellectuals and avant-garde thinkers. He frequently painted May, who had continued to model for him since his first portrait of her in 1920. *Au Cinquième: A Portrait of the Artist's Wife* (*Pl 9*) was painted in May's fifth floor flat and portrays her casually reading at the window, in strong contrast to Leech's first formal portrait of her. Leech captures the quiet domesticity and retiring lifestyle which they had adopted, and which he often recorded. *A Woman Darning* (National Gallery of Ireland) is one of a series of portraits of May, painted throughout the 1930s and 40s. These paintings not only show an intimist approach, they also mark the progression of time. One of the strengths of Leech's mature work is his composition, exemplified in *Au Cinquième: A Portrait of the Artist's Wife* by the strong diagonal of the window-sill repeated in May's raised left arm, on which her head and neck curve to rest on her hand. Sunlight and colour dominate the painting, and the same orange tones as found in the goose-girl's dress, painted about thirty years earlier, are repeated in May's sweater. Through the window is a view of the tall houses of Abbey Road.

While in London, Leech continued to paint landscapes, and in 1939 when Sydney Thompson visited him, they painted together at Billingsgate. Although Leech had exhibited yearly at the Royal Hibernian Academy, the Royal Academy, the Royal Institute of Oil Painters, the Royal Portrait Society, the New English Art

Club, and in various mixed exhibitions in England, he did not have an agent until 1944, when he was contacted by Mr Leo Smith, owner of the Dawson Gallery in Dublin. This resulted in a continuing friendship and led to three one-man shows at the Dawson Gallery: the first in June 1945, the second two years later and the third in 1951. Leech did not travel to Dublin for these exhibitions, but they advanced his reputation in Ireland. His style remained traditional, and though Leo Smith once had Leech's work exhibited at the Irish Exhibition of Living Art, Leech at this time had little sympathy for contemporary art. He complained: 'it is no joke battling against the popular stream of what goes for Art today', and he regarded some of his contemporaries as 'stunters' who were content to copy artists whom he admired, like Braque, Bonnard and Picasso. He regarded his own painting as 'honest and sincere works of art, which in years to come will turn out to be really good investments as well'. He looked carefully at the work of Cézanne which he felt had depth and mystery, and whose influence can be seen in his paintings of Regent's Park. *In Regent's Park* (Hugh Lane Municipal Gallery, Dublin), painted from a high perspective, captures the atmosphere of a summer's day. He painted many park views of overhanging reflected trees, bridges and people in boats, before and especially after the Second World War. He wrote in December 1950, 'The winter is a trying time now that I cannot go to the south of France, I work so much better and more easily from nature.'

During the Second World War Leech volunteered as a fire watcher, but when the blitz heightened in London and his Steele's Studio was damaged, he went with May to stay in Devon with his brother Cecil. They also spent some time in Guildford, becoming familiar with the Surrey landscape. Rivers, boats and reflections fascinated Leech, and May chauffeured him out into the countryside in her grey Austin 7. He painted *Boats on the Stour* by the river Stour, where Constable had painted. After 1947 he painted at Burley in the New Forest, producing *The Creek, Tuckton* (Drogheda Public Library), and he rekindled his friendship with Augustus John who lived nearby. He wrote in 1951, 'I got some good painting done at Burley and am now working in the Regent's Park again which is really lovely when it is fine.'

MARRIAGE TO MAY

'London is not what it was before the war, the kindliness has gone and the people changed, and also I have not been very well.' Both Leech and May Botterell wished to move out of London to a place in the country where they could live peacefully and where Leech could paint. Property had become scarce and expensive after the war, and it was not until 1958 that May's niece found Candy Cottage in West Clandon, outside Guildford. When Percy Botterell died in 1952 he left provision in his will for May, which enabled Bill and May to live comfortably after their marriage in 1953. Leech's first wife Elizabeth had died some years previously. This change gave Leech's painting a fresh impetus and in his new surroundings he painted works such as *A view on the Wey near Guildford* and *Clandon Station*, exemplifying this new energy. He built a studio in his garden and when the weather was fine he painted out of doors. He began his last great series of self-portraits, using a very large mirror, and again using his own paintings as background. This use of mirrors was a regular feature of his work, as it was with many of his contemporaries. Life was peaceful and easy for the couple, until May died in 1965. Leech then became very lonely and depressed. He continued to paint self-portraits, flowers, still lifes, and views out of his cottage window. His health was failing when, in July 1968, he fell off the railway bridge at West Clandon onto the track below and died later in hospital. Since he wished his paintings to be his epitaph, he requested that his ashes be scattered unceremoniously. In one of his last letters he wrote, 'You see not much success really, but you cannot be a recluse all your life as I have been and have worldly success. I had an idea when young, that if the work was good enough it would sell in the end.'